ESSENTIAL **DK**

GOOD PRACTICE

FILE
MANAGEMENT

ABOUT THIS BOOK

File Management is an easy-to-use guide that shows you
how to organize your documents more effectively, and how to
keep in control of the increasing number of files on your PC.

WHETHER YOU ARE A COMPLETE
beginner or are already using
Windows Me on a basic level,
the ability to manage the documents on
your computer efficiently is essential. This
book explains in simple terms how to view
the files on your computer, navigate
through the many levels of folders on your
hard disk, set up a personal filing system,
and maintain the good organization of
your documents in the future.

By working your way through the book
from the beginning and following the
tasks in sequence, you will achieve a
thorough understanding of the principles
involved in managing your files. At the
same time, the tasks that you complete
will prepare your computer for the next
time you come to save new documents.
Afterward, you can return to the
individual tasks and use them as a quick-
reference guide.

The chapters and the subsections present
the information using step-by-step

sequences. Virtually every step is
accompanied by an illustration showing
how your screen should look at each stage.

The book contains several features to
help you understand both what is
happening and what you need to do.

Command keys, such as ENTER and
CTRL, are shown in these rectangles:
Enter ↵ and Ctrl, so that there's no
confusion, for example, over whether
you should press that key or type the
letters "ctrl."

Cross-references are shown in the text as
left- or right-hand page icons: ◁ and ▷.
The page number and the reference are
shown at the foot of the page.

As well as the step-by-step sections,
there are boxes that explain a feature in
detail, and tip boxes that provide
alternative methods. Finally, at the back,
you will find a glossary of common terms,
and a comprehensive index.

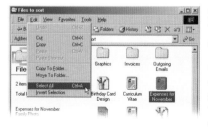

ESSENTIAL DK COMPUTERS

GOOD PRACTICE

FILE MANAGEMENT

ANDY ASHDOWN

LONDON, NEW YORK, MUNICH, MELBOURNE, DELHI

EDITOR Richard Gilbert
SENIOR ART EDITOR Sarah Cowley
DTP DESIGNER Rajen Shah
PRODUCTION CONTROLLER Sarah Sherlock

MANAGING EDITOR Adèle Hayward
MANAGING ART EDITOR Marianne Markham
CATEGORY PUBLISHER Stephanie Jackson

Produced for Dorling Kindersley Limited by
Design Revolution Limited, Queens Park Villa,
30 West Drive, Brighton, East Sussex BN2 0QW
EDITORIAL DIRECTOR Ian Whitelaw
SENIOR DESIGNER Andy Ashdown
PROJECT EDITOR John Watson
DESIGNER Andrew Easton

First published in Great Britain in 2000 by
Dorling Kindersley Limited,
80 Strand, London WC2R 0RL

Revised edition 2002

A Penguin Company

2 4 6 8 10 9 7 5 3 1

A CIP catalogue record for this book is available from the British Library.

ISBN 0-7513-6430-4

Colour reproduced by Colourscan, Singapore
Printed and bound in Italy by Graphicom

For our complete catalogue visit
www.dk.com

CONTENTS

MICROSOFT WINDOWS ME

Microsoft Windows has become the standard operating system for most personal computers, and you are likely to find it preinstalled on your home PC when you unpack it from its box.

WHAT IS WINDOWS ME?

Windows Me is simply an operating system – the interface between you and the work you create on your computer. Microsoft Windows has played a key part in transforming the way we view computing, simplifying the whole process so that you no longer have to understand confusing computer code to make things work. It is designed so that the operations you carry out become familiar, no matter which program is running; and remember that working with Windows is just like working conventionally. You will find items that you would expect to see at your desk, for example, a wastebasket and a folder called **My Documents** for your files.

COMPUTING MADE SIMPLE

If you are a newcomer to Windows, try not to be daunted by all the icons, menus, and numerous options. Keep things simple and think about what you would do if you were holding a piece of paper in your hand rather than manipulating a computer file. If you want to throw a file away, then you put it in the recycle bin. If you want to save it for future reference, then you place it into a folder.

Windows are exactly that – boxes that allow you to "see into" the locations on your computer where files are saved. From within these windows you can manage your files by performing certain actions.

THE WINDOWS ME DESKTOP

The screen that is displayed when your computer has started up is known as the "desktop." Just like the desk in your study or office, this is the place where you will find everything at hand so that you can carry out whatever tasks need to be done.

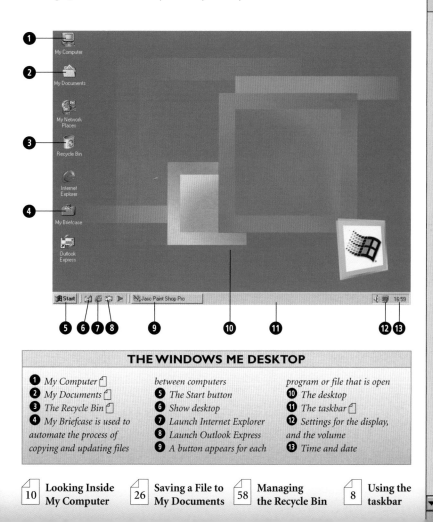

THE WINDOWS ME DESKTOP

❶ *My Computer* 🗋
❷ *My Documents* 🗋
❸ *The Recycle Bin* 🗋
❹ *My Briefcase is used to automate the process of copying and updating files*

between computers
❺ *The Start button*
❻ *Show desktop*
❼ *Launch Internet Explorer*
❽ *Launch Outlook Express*
❾ *A button appears for each*

program or file that is open
❿ *The desktop*
⓫ *The taskbar* 🗋
⓬ *Settings for the display, and the volume*
⓭ *Time and date*

USING THE TASKBAR

The taskbar is the long gray panel that runs along the bottom of your screen. As well as containing the **Start** button, where you launch programs and access other functions, it also displays a button for each window or file that you have open. By clicking on a button you are taken immediately to that particular window and, as you have more files open and programs running simultaneously, this panel becomes an easy way to navigate your way around. The taskbar can become cramped at its current (default) size because the buttons become smaller as you open more windows. You may want to alter the taskbar's shape to see the buttons in the larger size, or move the taskbar to an entirely new position on the desktop.

1 SELECTING THE TASKBAR
● Position your cursor over the top edge of the taskbar so that it turns into a double-headed arrow.

2 INCREASING THE TASKBAR SIZE
● Hold down the left mouse button and drag the edge of the taskbar higher up the screen.
● When the taskbar is large enough, release the mouse button to set the taskbar to its new size.
● If at any time you want to reduce the size of the taskbar, or return it to its original position, simply select it as before and drag it down the screen.

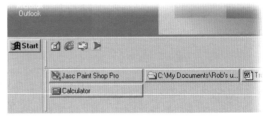

3 MOVING THE TASKBAR

● In addition to changing the size of the taskbar, you can also alter its position. It may suit you better to work with the taskbar positioned at the top of the screen or down either side.

● To move the taskbar to a new position, first place the mouse cursor on any clear area in the gray panel.

● Hold down the left mouse button and move the cursor to your preferred location until you see a temporary outline that indicates where the taskbar will appear.

An outline appears to indicate ●
where the taskbar will move to

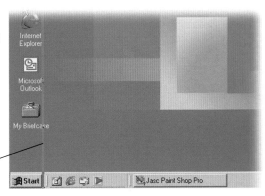

● Release the mouse button and the taskbar moves to its new position. The icons on your desktop reposition themselves to accommodate the relocated taskbar.

VIEWING YOUR FILES

Managing files is easy once you are familiar with how they appear on your computer. There are many different ways to view files, and you can adopt a preference that suits you.

LOOKING INSIDE MY COMPUTER

All of the programs and files on your computer are stored on the hard disk: **Local Disk** (C:). This is located in the **My**

Computer icon – the main "entrance" into your PC. Here you will also find access to the floppy disk and CD-ROM drives.

OPENING MY COMPUTER

● Position your cursor over the **My Computer** icon in the top left corner of the Windows desktop.
● Double-click the left mouse button and the **My Computer** window opens. Note that the taskbar now displays a button for the open window.

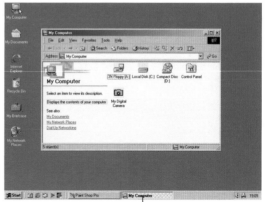

Clicking on this taskbar button will return you to the window at any time

| 8 | Using the Taskbar |

The floppy disk drive

Your computer's hard disk, where the programs and files on your computer are stored

The CD-ROM drive

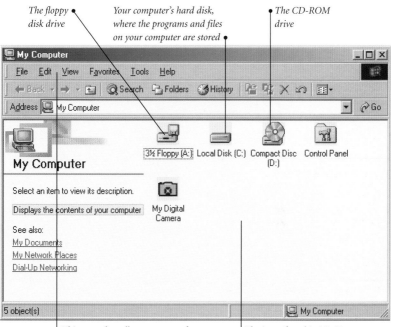

• *This menu bar allows you to perform a variety of functions within the window*

• *The items found in My Computer are displayed in this area of the window*

MINIMIZING, MAXIMIZING, AND CLOSING A WINDOW

The three buttons in the top right of an open window control how it appears onscreen. Clicking on the minimize button (–) makes the window disappear, but you will see a button remain on the taskbar. The maximize button (□) makes the window fill the

screen. You can click on it again to restore the window to its original size. The (X) button closes the window.

RESIZING A WINDOW

You can make a window larger or smaller by clicking in the bottom right corner and dragging the window to a new size.

VIEWING FILES IN WINDOWS

The default setting for Windows Me is to display the contents of open windows as large icons, showing nothing more than the name of the file and an icon to indicate its file type ⬜. However, there are many ways to organize and view items within windows by changing the appearance of files, and by arranging them in a particular order.

1 SELECTING AUTO ARRANGE

● A window's contents displayed as large icons can often appear disordered, but you can arrange a window's contents by using **Auto Arrange**.

● Folders created in the **My Documents** folder may display their contents in this disorganized way, so open this window by double-clicking on its icon.

● With a "messy" folder open, select **Arrange Icons** from the **View** menu and choose **Auto Arrange** from the submenu.

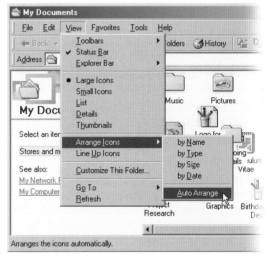

2 THE CONTENTS REARRANGED

● The menu closes and the icons rearrange themselves neatly within the window. With the **Auto Arrange** feature left on, the icons always automatically align themselves with one another when you resize a window or add new folders.

23 **File Name Extensions and File Icons**

3 ARRANGING IN OTHER WAYS

● As well as arranging icons automatically, it is also possible to arrange the icons by **Name**, **Type**, **Size**, or **Date** – just as you can by sorting files in **Details** mode △.

● Experiment by using the same procedure as **Auto Arrange**, but select one of the other options under **Arrange Icons** option in the **View** menu.

● In this example the items are arranged by their size.

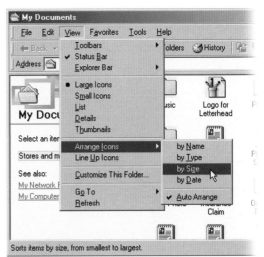

Menu options...

Wherever relevant, the steps in this section show you how to select options from the menus found at the top of open windows. Often, many of these functions are also available by clicking on the right mouse button within a window, or by using a keyboard shortcut. By experimenting, you will become more familiar with your computer and develop methods of performing these tasks with which you feel most comfortable.

LINING UP THE CONTENTS OF A WINDOW

Under the **View** menu you will also see an option called **Line Up Icons**. This performs the same action as arranging the icons, but not in any order. This option aligns the icons into columns and rows by moving them slightly from their current positions.

4 VIEWING AS SMALL ICONS

● Next, we are going to look at changing the appearance of the information that is displayed in a window.

● Return to the **My Computer** window .
Its contents are currently displayed as large icons.

● Click on **View** in the menu bar, and in the drop-down menu you will see that the current option – **Large Icons** – is indicated as being selected by a black circle, known as a bullet.

● Place the mouse cursor over the **Small Icons** option and click once.

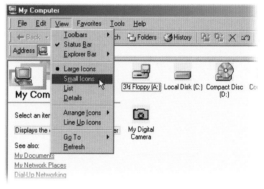

● The icons in the window change to the smaller size and realign themselves into tighter columns.

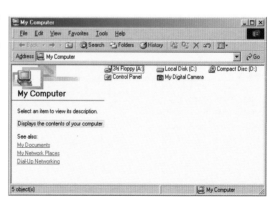

5 VIEWING AS A LIST

● Display the **View** menu again, but this time select **List** from the options.

● The contents retain their small icons, but now appear as a list arranged vertically in the window.

6 VIEWING DETAILS

● Now select **Details** from the **View** menu.

● When you select this option, certain information appears alongside the icons such as **Type** and **Total Size**.

● Later, when you start to view windows containing individual files and folders in this way, you will also see their modification date.

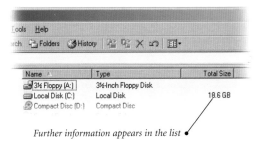

Further information appears in the list ●

ORGANIZING A WINDOW'S CONTENTS

When you view the contents of a window in **Details** mode, you will see that a series of small boxes appears along the top of the open window containing headings for each category of information shown. By clicking on these headings you can reorganize the contents of the window into different lists according to different criteria.

1 ORGANIZING FILES BY NAME

● To explore the different ways of organizing your files in **Details** mode, double-click on **Local Disk** (C:). Here, you will be able see the effect of reorganizing the files and folders that are listed.

● When the **Local Disk** (C:) window opens, display the **View** menu and select **Details**.

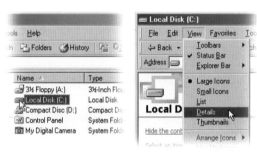

● Windows Me automatically sorts the items listed under the **Name** heading into alphabetical order. Folders are always shown at the top of the list, with individual files listed below.

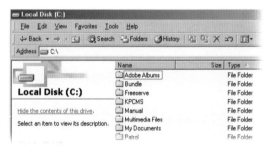

● By clicking once on the **Name** heading box, you can view the items in reverse alphabetical order, which also places the folders in the window after the list of individual files.

2 ORGANIZING FILES BY SIZE

● You can view items listed by size by clicking on the **Size** heading box at the top.

● The files are listed with the smallest shown at the top, folders are again grouped at the top.

● Click again on the **Size** heading box if you want to view the files listed in reverse size order.

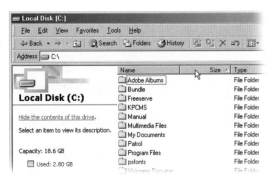

3 ORGANIZING FILES BY TYPE

● Click on the **Type** heading box.

● The items in the window are grouped according to their different types, which are listed alphabetically.

● As before, you can click again on the heading box to view the groups in reverse alphabetical order.

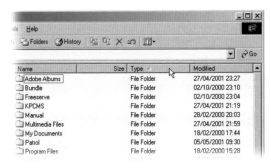

4 ORGANIZING FILES BY DATE

● Click on the **Modified** heading box.

● The files and folders are reordered so that the oldest items are shown at the top of the list.

● If you want to view the newest files, click again on the heading box. The date order of the list is reversed.

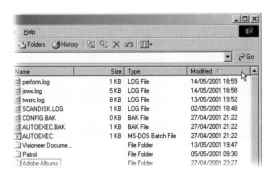

VIEWING FILES IN WINDOWS EXPLORER

The last few pages have shown you the basic methods for viewing files within open windows. However, Windows Me has an additional tool, Windows Explorer, which provides you with another means of viewing and managing your files. It allows you to do all the same things that you would do by using Windows conventionally, but also shows you exactly where a file is saved by guiding you visually through the hierarchy of folders on your computer's hard disk.

1 LAUNCHING EXPLORER

● To launch Windows Explorer, click once on the **Start** button in the bottom left corner of the taskbar ⌐|.

● Choose **Programs** from the pop-up menu, followed by **Accessories**. Then select **Windows Explorer** from the submenu that appears at the side.

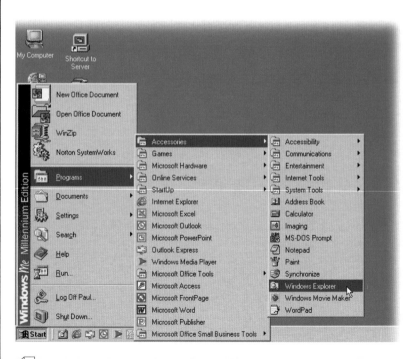

● Either release the mouse button, or left-click, and Windows Explorer opens.

● By default, the window displays the contents of the **My Documents** folder.

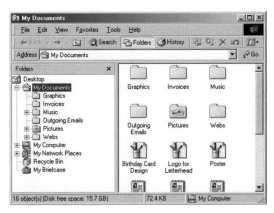

● To make the window fill the screen, click on the **Maximize** button □.

RESIZING THE WINDOW PANELS

If the folders displayed in the left-hand panel are obscured, place the cursor over the gray vertical bar that divides the two parts of the window. The cursor changes to a double-headed arrow. Hold down the mouse button and drag the bar to the right. When the left-hand panel is sufficiently large to reveal the list of folders, release the mouse button.

11 Minimizing, Maximizing, and Closing a Window

NAVIGATING WITH EXPLORER

When you first launch Windows Explorer, a diagram is displayed in the left-hand panel listing items that branch from the **Desktop** – the top level of your computer. You will see that **My Documents** is automatically highlighted in the list because this is where the majority of the folders and files that you would usually access are stored. The folders that the disk contains are listed below its name. As the disk is highlighted, its contents appear automatically in the panel to the right. Note that individual files are not shown in the list to the left, but they do appear along with the folders in the main panel. By following the connecting lines in the diagram, you can see that **Pictures** is stored in **My Documents,** which, in turn, can be found on the **Desktop**.

• Many options appear as buttons in a menu bar

• The left-hand panel displays a diagram showing the hierarchy of all the drives and folders on your computer

• When a folder or drive in the left-hand diagram is highlighted, the files and folders it contains appear in the panel to the right

WHY USE WINDOWS EXPLORER?

It is purely personal preference whether you want to use Windows Explorer to manage your files. With Explorer, you can perform all the operations – copying , renaming , and deleting  – that you might carry out across open windows. The main advantage of using Windows Explorer is the ability to navigate your way through the entire contents of your computer within a single open window. This avoids constantly opening and closing different windows, or having a number of windows open at the same time.

FOLDERS WITHIN FOLDERS

In the diagram, you will see that many folders have a small square next to them containing either a plus symbol (+) or a minus symbol (–). This is a quick way of seeing whether a folder contains other folders that aren't currently displayed. A plus sign (+) next to a folder means that it contains other folders (known as subfolders), but they are not presently displayed in the diagram. A minus symbol (–) next to a folder shows that it is open and other folders it contains are listed in the diagram. If there is no symbol next to a folder, there are no other folders inside it. This does not necessarily mean that the folder is empty, as it could still contain individual files.

2 REVEALING THE SUBFOLDERS

● Position the cursor over one of the squares in the diagram that contains a plus symbol (+) and left-click once.

● A new list of folders appears underneath, branching from the folder you selected, and the plus symbol (+) changes to a minus symbol (–).

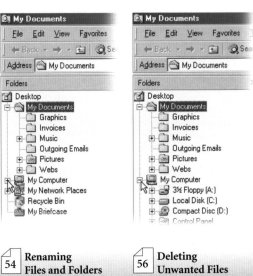

47	**Copying Files to Other Locations**
54	**Renaming Files and Folders**
56	**Deleting Unwanted Files**

3 REVEAL FOLDER CONTENTS

● To see all the files that the folder contains, click once on the folder that you just clicked next to.

● The folder becomes highlighted and its contents are displayed in the main right-hand panel.

The contents of the folder are displayed in this panel

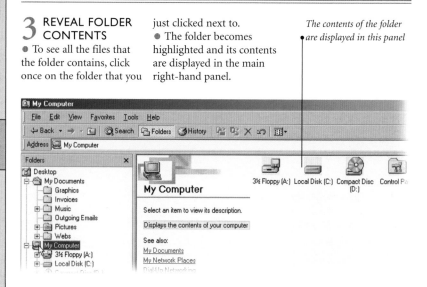

4 HIDING THE SUBFOLDERS

● Place the cursor over the square that now contains a minus symbol (–) and left-click once.

● The folders that stem from your selected folder disappear, and the symbol in the square becomes a plus sign (+) again.

FILE NAME EXTENSIONS AND FILE ICONS

Whenever you save a file, three letters are added to the name, which indicate its file type. This is known as a file name extension, but it isn't always visible. In addition, the file is also given a graphic symbol called an icon – which is always visible – so you can instantly recognize the file type, or the program used to create it.

VIEWING THE FILE EXTENSIONS

● Open a window that contains some of your files and select **Folder Options** from the **Tools** menu. Under the **View** tab, click in the square next to **Hide file extensions for known file types** to remove the check mark. When you click on **OK**, the extensions appear after the file names.

Logo for Letterhead....

Poster.bmp

Curriculum Vitae.doc

FILE NAME EXTENSIONS

Here are some common extensions that you may see following the names of files that you save:

.doc Word/WordPad document

.xls Excel spreadsheet

.txt Text document

.psp Paint Shop Pro image file

.tif Tagged Image File Format

.png Portable Network Graphic file

COMMON FILE ICONS

Files are given a unique icon depending on the program they were created in. These icons provide you with a simple way of distinguishing text files from graphics files, and so on.

 A document created in WordPad

 A graphics file created in Paint

 A document created in Microsoft Word

 A spreadsheet created in Microsoft Excel

 An image file created in Paint Shop Pro

The standard Windows icon

OPENING AND SAVING

These two operations are among the first that you will carry out on your computer. However simple they may seem, saving your files correctly is a crucial part of good file management.

OPENING FILES FROM A WINDOW

A common way of opening documents is first to open the program used to create it, and then select **Open** from the **File** menu. However, a simpler way to open a file is to locate it on your computer (using the navigation techniques described in the previous chapter) and open it directly from the folder window containing the file.

1 SELECTING A FILE TO OPEN
● Open the window of the folder containing the file that you wish to open.
● Click once on the file icon to highlight it.

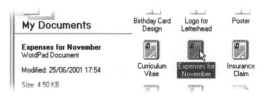

2 OPENING THE FILE
● Click on **File** in the Menu bar at the top of the window and select **Open** from the drop-down menu.
● The program that was used to create the file launches automatically, and the file you selected opens onscreen.

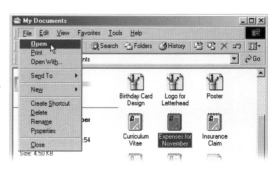

OPENING A RECENT FILE

Windows Me contains a feature that allows most programs to add files to a list of up to 15 files in the Start menu. These are the files that you have been working on most recently. This feature provides a quick and easy way of opening a recent file.

1 OPENING FROM THE START MENU

● Click once on the Start button in the bottom left corner of the taskbar ⌐.
● Choose Documents from the pop-up menu. You will see that your most recent files are listed in the submenu that appears.
● Highlight a file and release the mouse button.
● As before, the program launches and your chosen file opens.

The most recent files that you have been working on appear in this list

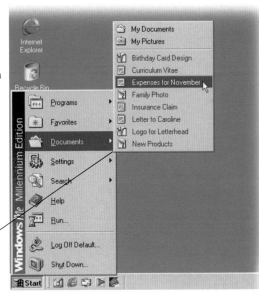

OPENING FILES THE QUICK WAY

Once you gain confidence in handling files within their windows, the easiest, and by far the quickest, way to open them is by simply double-clicking on the file icon. Within an open window, double-click on the file icon (there is no need to highlight it first by selecting it). The program launches and the file opens to be worked on.

SAVING A FILE TO MY DOCUMENTS

Although saving is a very simple process, it is not without its pitfalls. If you don't have logical locations on your computer to save your files, you can soon create filing havoc on your computer's hard disk. The next few steps show the default location of your files when you save them, and how you can modify that location.

1 CREATING A NEW DOCUMENT

● Before you can familiarize yourself with saving files, you first need to create a new document with which to experiment. If the document from the previous task is open, then close it and create a new file.

● In the example shown below, we are using a new document created in WordPad, which is a simple word processing program that comes with Windows Me. It can be found in the **Start** menu under **Programs** and then under **Accessories**.

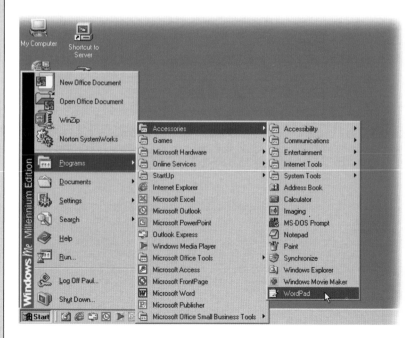

2 SELECTING SAVE AS

● With the new WordPad document open, click on **File** in the Menu bar and select **Save As** from the drop-down menu.

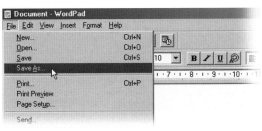

3 SELECTING THE LOCATION

● The **Save As** dialog box opens. At the top there is a text box with the words **Save in** written alongside. This is where you select the location in which to save your document.

● The current location shown in the box is **My Documents**. Your computer automatically selects this location when you open a program and select **Save** or **Save As** for the first time.

● Any other folders that are also contained in this location are displayed in the window. Although you can choose to save the document loose in **My Documents**, try placing it into one of the existing folders by double-clicking on the folder's icon. If there are no folders, you can create a new one in which the document can be saved 🗋.

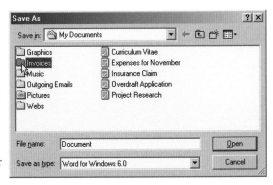

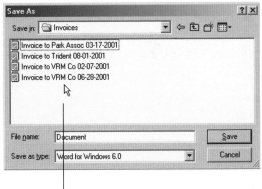

● *Double-clicking on a folder displays its contents in the window, and selects it as the new location*

35 **Creating New Folders as You Save**

4 NAMING THE DOCUMENT

● Click in the **File name** text box at the start of the default name (**Document**). The cursor changes to a blinking insertion bar.

● Hold down the mouse button and drag the insertion bar over the name to highlight it.

● Type in the new name.

5 SAVING THE DOCUMENT

● Click on the **Save** button and your document is saved to your preferred location.

● Close the program and check that the file has been saved to the correct location by opening the folder window containing your document.

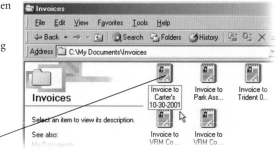

The file has been saved in your chosen location

I Can't See the My Documents Folder on the Desktop…

If for any reason the **My Documents** folder doesn't appear on your desktop,

then it can be found within **My Computer** ⬚. Double-click on the **My Computer** icon on the desktop to view its contents. The main drives of your computer

(the floppy disk drive, the hard disk, and the CD-ROM drive) appear in the list. Double-click on **Local Disk (C:)** and you will see the **My Documents** folder.

CHANGING THE FILE TYPE

When you save a file for the first time, the program that you are running saves the document as a specific file type 🗋, usually a basic format recognized only by that particular program. However, it is possible to change the file type of the document you are saving so that it can be recognized by other software packages or a different computer operating system (such as the Apple Macintosh system, for example).

1 OPEN THE SAVE AS DIALOG BOX
● Save a file through the **Save As** dialog box as usual 🗋, choosing its location and giving the document a name. Before you save, click on the arrow next to the **Save as type** box to see a list of file type options.

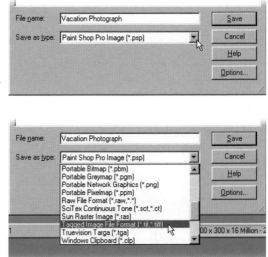

2 SELECTING THE FILE TYPE
● In this example we are going to save a Paint Shop Pro image file as a TIFF (**Tagged Image File Format**).
● Highlight this option in the list and click on **Save**.

SELECTING A FILE TYPE FOR TEXT DOCUMENTS

The most common format for transferring text documents is **Text Only**. Although this format is widely recognized, be aware that it will remove the formatting (indents, text styling, etc) from your document, and strip it down to simple unformatted text. Because of this, it makes more sense to save your text documents in a standard format, then make a copy (saved as **Text Only**) to use for file transfer.

YOUR FILING SYSTEM

The key to good file management is not only understanding where files on your computer are stored – you also need to develop your own system for saving files in organized folders.

BETTER FILE MANAGEMENT

You can, if you want, save your documents loose within the **My Documents** folder. However, as you create more files, the folder will soon become very full and disorganized, and you will begin to lose track of what each file contains. This can be time-consuming and frustrating when you want to return to documents. The next few pages take you through all the steps involved in setting up a filing system.

KEEPING IT ORGANIZED

You will be surprised by just how many files you create as you begin to use your computer's potential. In addition to simple word processing and spreadsheets, you may also want to create graphics and pictures by using image-based software. If you are connected to the internet, you will want to save emails, as well as files that you download, for future reference. Not only will you be doing all these things as a home user, you may also be creating documents that are work-related. If you have two or three family members using the PC for their own purposes, you will soon begin to understand why good file manage-ment is essential.

From searching the world wide web to juggling home finances, from drawing images to business matters, all the files you create need to be stored sensibly.

DESIGNING YOUR NEW FILING SYSTEM

It is essential to start using a logical system for saving your files as soon as possible. It is easy to overlook this in your haste to "play" with your new PC, but it will be a long and arduous task to return and organize all those files later. Before creating a filing system on the computer, begin by planning it on paper.

1 WHO WILL BE USING YOUR PC?

● First, make a list of all the people who will be using your computer. In the case of a home PC, this is likely to be the members of your household.

● These people become first-level entries in your new filing system.

● Even if you are the only person using your computer, still put your name at the top of the list.

their own personal projects.

● These categories become second-level entries in the system.

2 WHAT WILL THEY BE USING IT FOR?

● Each person that uses your PC will do so for a variety of reasons.

● Against each user's name, list the categories of the different types of work that they are likely to undertake. These might include work, personal projects, home finances, college, etc. You may have to repeat some of the categories, for example, most of the users will have

My new filing system

Gary
- Work:
- Personal Projects: Expenses, Invoicing, E
- Internet: Digital Photography
My Web Site, Down

- Home Finances: Bank Account, M

Melanie

3 LIST SPECIFIC PROJECTS

● Next to each category, make a third-level list of more specific projects or jobs relevant to the particular category.

● The entries in this third level will eventually become folders to contain all the text documents, graphics, emails, and other files that are associated with a particular job or project.

● This level will constantly expand, but begin by listing as many specific projects as possible that are already on your computer.

YOUR FINAL DESIGN

This is a modified illustration, based on how Windows Explorer might represent your new filing system, showing the levels in your design as folders. Later, we will be creating all the folders shown in the diagram on your computer. These folders will form the basis of your filing system.

The main folder: *where your filing system will be stored*

Level one folders: *for each user*

Level two folders: *for project categories*

Level three folders: *to contain documents*

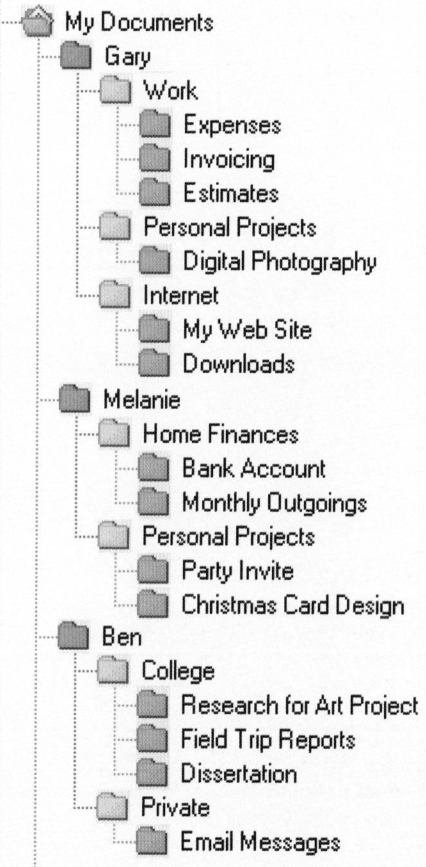

My Documents
Gary
Work
Expenses
Invoicing
Estimates
Personal Projects
Digital Photography
Internet
My Web Site
Downloads
Melanie
Home Finances
Bank Account
Monthly Outgoings
Personal Projects
Party Invite
Christmas Card Design
Ben
College
Research for Art Project
Field Trip Reports
Dissertation
Private
Email Messages

All documents associated with a particular project or job should be stored within individual third-level folders

Just the beginning…
Remember that this is just the starting point for your new filing system. Over time, you will need to modify your use of folders, indeed you will certainly have to create many more levels of subfolders to store individual projects. Where you choose to save your files is not set in stone, and you can easily modify your system later by moving files and folders to new locations.

45 **Moving Files Between Locations**

CREATING NEW FOLDERS

A folder on your computer should be used to store files that are associated with one another. This means that all your documents are kept in logical groups and are easy to find. In order to create your filing system, you will need to make a number of new folders on your PC, in which you can place your files. You can create as many folders and subfolders as you wish, and you should develop the habit of creating a new folder for each new job or project that you undertake.

1 OPENING MY DOCUMENTS

● We are going to use the existing folder, **My Documents**, as the location for housing your new filing system.

● Double-click on the **My Documents** icon on the desktop.
● The **My Documents** window opens. There are some standard folders that will already exist in this location, including **Pictures, Music,** and **Webs.**
● If you are not using your computer for the first time, there are also likely to be some other existing files, and possibly folders, saved in the **My Documents** folder as well. These will have to be organized into your new filing system, but for now we are going to put them all out of the way into one folder so that you can return and sort through them later.

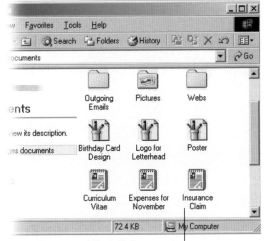

*Your **My Documents** folder is likely to contain a number of disorganized files and folders*

2 CREATING A NEW FOLDER

● Within the window of the **My Documents** folder, click on the **File** menu. Select **New**, followed by **Folder** at the top of the submenu.

● A new folder appears in the **My Documents** window.

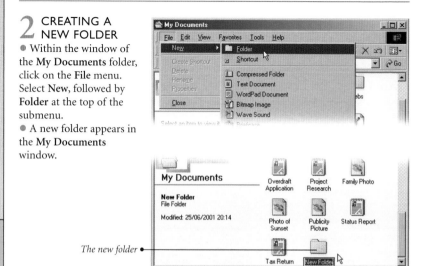

The new folder ●

3 NAMING THE NEW FOLDER

● With the new folder highlighted, type in a new name, **Files to sort**. Press the Enter ← key and deselect the folder by clicking once in any blank area of the window.

● You have now created a new folder that is ready to be used to store all those disorganized files.

● To keep the window neat while you create your new filing system, we are going to place the files and folders, currently saved in **My Documents**, into the new folder.

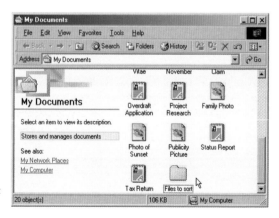

4 PUT AWAY YOUR EXISTING FILES

● Click on an existing file and keep the mouse button held down. The file becomes highlighted.

● Move the file into the new folder by dragging the icon over the folder and releasing the mouse button. The file is now placed in the folder.

● Repeat this process for each of the files and folders in the window. If there are a number of items to move, refer to the section dealing with making multiple selections 🖰. You can leave the standard folders – **Pictures, Music,** and **Webs** – where they are.

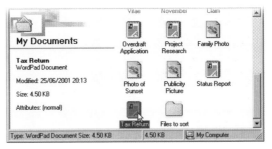

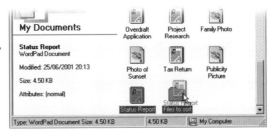

CREATING NEW FOLDERS AS YOU SAVE

Another way to make new folders is to create them at the same time as saving a document. You will find this a useful feature once your new filing system is in place because you can create folders for new projects as you save documents, rather than preparing them in advance. When you select **Save As**, to save a document for the first time 🖰, select a location for your file as normal,

but do not click on **Save** immediately. Instead, click once on the **Create New Folder** button – a new

Create New Folder button ●

folder appears in the list. The folder's name is automatically highlighted so that you have the opportunity to give it a more specific name. Once you have typed in the folder's new name, double-click on it to select the folder, then name the new document by typing it into the **File Name** box. When you click on the **Save** button, the document is saved into your new folder.

| 42 | Selecting Your Files |

| 26 | Saving a File to My Documents |

CREATING YOUR NEW FILING SYSTEM

We are now going to continue creating new folders within **My Documents** to set up the filing system you designed on page 31. The following steps also show you how to create folders within folders, which are known as subfolders.

1 CREATING YOUR MAIN FOLDERS

● Other than the standard folders, there should now only be one folder currently in view in the **My Documents** window, named **Files to sort**, which contains all the files and folders that were already saved in this location. Make sure that it is not selected by clicking on any blank area in the window.

● Click on **File** in the Menu bar. Select **New** from the top of the drop-down menu, and **Folder** from the submenu.

● Give the new folder the name of one of your computer users from the top level of your design, in this case – **Gary**.

● Continue to create new folders for each of the users, naming each of the folders as you create them.

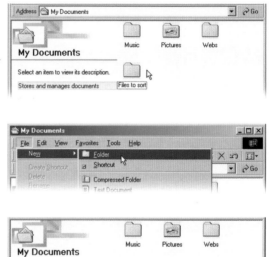

2 CREATE A USER'S SUBFOLDERS

● We are now going to place a series of folders within the user's main folder, corresponding to the second level in the design.

● Select a user's folder by double-clicking on its icon in the window. A new window opens to reveal the contents of that particular folder which, of course, is currently empty. Any folders that you now create are saved directly into that user's folder.

● Create a folder in the new window in the usual way and give it a category name, in this case – **Work**.

● Make new folders for each of the categories listed underneath this particular user in the second level of your design.

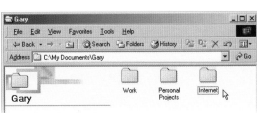

3 FURTHER SUBFOLDERS

● Before repeating the above process for each of the other users, first complete the filing system for your currently selected user. In the same way as shown in step 2, you need to create further subfolders within the category folders you have just made. These will correspond to the third level in your design.

● Double-click on a category folder to view its contents.

● In the new window, create new folders for each of the third-level entries under the currently selected category.

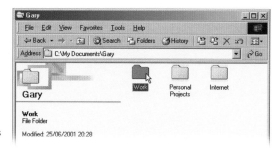

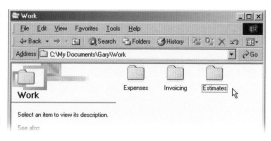

4 MOVING TO THE NEXT CATEGORY

● To create third-level folders in the remaining second-level categories, you will need to return to view the contents of your current user in level one.

● Keep clicking on the **Back** button in the menu bar until you return to the window that displays the folders for each second-level category.

● Double-click on the next category to open its window.

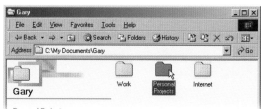

● Create the third-level folders for this category.
● Repeat step 4 for each second-level category.

5 MOVING TO THE NEXT USER

● Having completed the filing system for one user, you need to repeat the process for each of the others. Remember that the window will currently display the contents of a second-level subfolder for your first user.

● Return to your first level of folders by clicking on the **Back** button.

● Repeat steps 2 to 5 for each of the people listed in the design of your filing system.

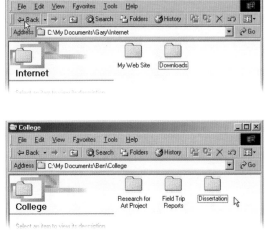

See your filing system in all its glory…

Remember that once you have completed your filing system, you can check its complete structure by viewing it through Windows Explorer ⌐.

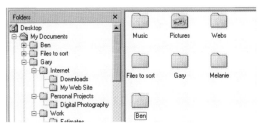

CREATING A SHORTCUT TO A FOLDER

If there is a particular folder, or folders, in your filing system that you need to access regularly, then it may be worth creating a shortcut on the desktop. A shortcut made from a folder acts as a direct link taking you directly to an open window for that particular folder, instead of having to "drill down" through many levels of folders to reach it. With this in mind, a shortcut can become a valuable time-saving device if your chosen folder is buried within many levels of subfolders.

1 CHOOSING THE FOLDER
● Open the window that contains the folder you wish to create a shortcut to.
● Click once on your chosen folder so that it is highlighted.

2 CREATING THE SHORTCUT
● Click on **File** in the menu bar at the top of the open window. In the drop-down menu, click once on **Send To**, then click on **Desktop (create shortcut)** in the submenu.

Selecting this option instead creates a shortcut in the same location

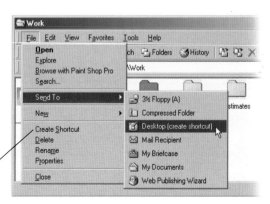

3 YOUR SHORTCUT IS CREATED

● Close the window and the shortcut that you created appears on the desktop. Shortcuts are distinguished by a small arrow in the bottom left-hand corner of the icon.

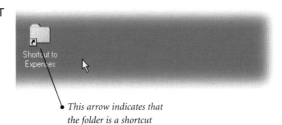

This arrow indicates that the folder is a shortcut

4 OPENING FROM A SHORTCUT

● To open the folder linked to the shortcut, simply double-click on the shortcut's folder icon.

● The window for that specific folder opens immediately.

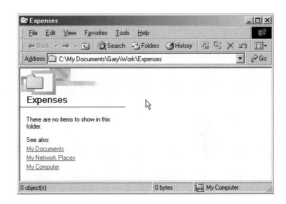

SHORTCUTS FOR FILES AND PROGRAMS

You can create shortcuts for individual files and programs in the same way as folders. Be careful about this though. You may have just created a thoroughly efficient filing system on your computer, but creating too many shortcuts can very quickly make an unusable mess of your desktop!

MOVING AND COPYING

An important part of organizing your files is the ability to move and copy your documents between different locations within your filing system.

SELECTING YOUR FILES

Moving and copying both use simple "drag and drop" techniques that involve picking up a file, or folder, from one open window and placing it into another. For this to happen, you need first to select the files that you want to move. You can select individual files, or several at a time. To become familiar with the different methods of selecting, we are going to organize all the files that you stored under **Files to sort** earlier in the book ⌐. If you don't have some old files to organize, the following steps are equally as relevant for selecting and moving files in the future.

1 SELECTING A SINGLE FILE
● Open the window to display the contents of the **Files to sort** folder.
● Within this window you should see a variety of files and folders, as shown here.
● To select a file, click once on its icon in the window. The file becomes highlighted to show that it is now selected.

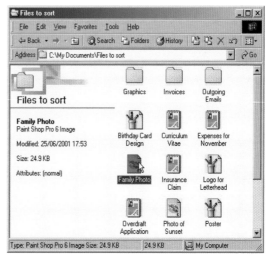

2 SELECTING GROUPS OF FILES

● You can continue to select further files that are positioned next to your currently selected file.

● With the file still selected, place the cursor over the next file to be selected.

● Hold down the ⇧ Shift key and now, when you click on your second file, both are highlighted.

● Holding down the ⇧ Shift key can also be used to select files in a block by clicking on two files that occupy the opposite corners of a grid.

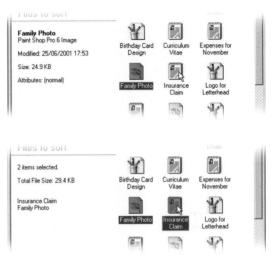

3 SELECTING UNGROUPED FILES

● You can select several files from the window, even if they are not positioned next to one another.

● Click on any empty area of the window to deselect any highlighted files.

● Select your first file, as described in step 1.

● Hold down the Ctrl key and click on a second file anywhere in the window, both files become highlighted.

● Keep the Ctrl key held down to select further files.

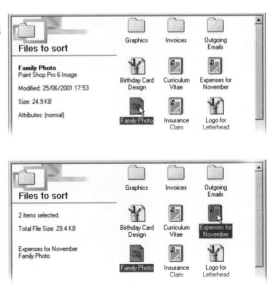

4 SELECTING ALL FILES

● To select all the items in an open window, click on **Edit** in the menu bar. Choose **Select All** from the drop-down menu.

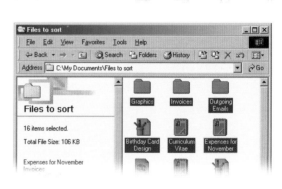

● When you release the mouse button, the menu closes and the entire contents of the window are highlighted.

5 DESELECTING FILES

● To deselect a single file from this group of selected files, hold down the Ctrl key.

● Click on the file that you would like to deselect. You will see that it is no longer highlighted.

● Keep the Ctrl key held down to deselect further files.

INVERTING A SELECTION

You can reverse which files are selected and deselected by choosing **Invert Selection** from the **Edit** menu within the window. When you select this option every file that is currently highlighted will become deselected and the files that are deselected become highlighted.

MOVING FILES BETWEEN LOCATIONS

We are now going to use the selection methods described in the previous task to move your existing files into your new filing system. When you move a file, it means that the place where that file is saved on your computer changes from one location to another. This is different from copying, where the file that you copy and move can result in copies being stored in any number of locations.

1 CHOOSING THE FILES TO MOVE

● Open the window of the **Files to sort** folder to display its contents.
● Decide which file(s) you are going to move first, for example, all files that are connected by belonging to one of the users.
● In this case, we are going to move all the photographic files that belong to Gary into the relevant folder in the filing system.

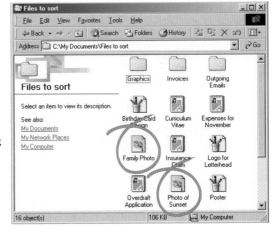

2 CHOOSING THE NEW LOCATION

● Select the files that are to be moved.
● Click on the **Edit** in the menu bar and select **Move To Folder**.

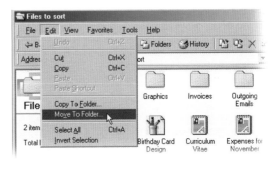

| 31 | Designing Your New Filing System |
| 47 | Copying Files to Other Locations |

● The **Browse For Folder** window opens.

● Before you move a file, you need to decide where you want to move it to. The files that we have chosen belong in the new folder called **Digital Photography**, found within Gary's own set of folders.

● Navigate to this folder using the techniques shown on pages 18–19 📄, and click on the folder to select it.

● Click on the **OK** button.

Browse For Folder ?X

Move the selected item(s) to the folder:

- ⊟ 🖳 My Documents
  - ⊞ 🗀 Ben
  - ⊞ 🗀 Files to sort
  - ⊟ 🗀 Gary
    - ⊞ 🗀 Internet
    - ⊟ 🗀 Personal Projects
      - 📁 Digital Photography
    - ⊞ 🗀 Work

Folder: Digital Photography

[OK] [Cancel] [New Folder]

3 VIEWING THE MOVED FILES

● The files will move from one location to the other.

● You can check this by opening the window for the new location. The files will be visible in the window.

Digital Photography

File Edit View Favorites Tools Help

← Back ▾ → ▾ 🖭 | 🔍 Search 🗀 Folders 🕙 History | 🖳 🖳 ✕

Address 🗀 C:\My Documents\Gary\Personal Projects\Digital Photography

Digital Photography   Family Photo   Photo of Sunset

Continue sorting…
Check your computer for files that may have been accidentally saved to other locations on your hard drive and move these into your filing system as well.

BEWARE OF WHAT YOU MOVE

Although moving your own files around your computer is a simple task, don't be tempted to start "organizing" other aspects of your computer's hard drive. To make everything work properly, the operating system "knows" where important system files are stored, and uses these to launch the programs that you run on your computer. If you inadvertently move files that the computer requires, you can expect a time-consuming, and possibly expensive, process to fix it. This is why it is safest to restrict all your file management to the **My Documents** folder.

COPYING FILES TO OTHER LOCATIONS • 47

COPYING FILES TO OTHER LOCATIONS

The process of copying files is similar to moving them – however, the original file remains in place and a duplicate file appears in a new location. The main reason why you would want to copy files to different locations on your computer is to create backups in case anything goes wrong with your original file. Remember

though, copying is not like making a shortcut 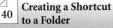 because when you make a copy, both files become independent of one another, whereas a shortcut is only a link to the original. This means that changes you make to the original file are not reflected in a copy until you overwrite it with a new copy.

1 CHOOSING THE FILE TO COPY

● Let's assume that you already have a file saved on your computer that needs to be located in two different folders within your new filing system. During your reorganization, the file will have been moved into one of the relevant folders.
● Open the window containing the file you wish to copy and select it.

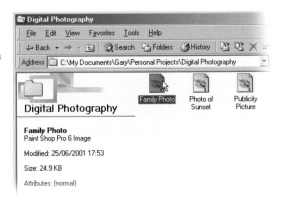

2 COPYING THE FILE

● Select **Copy To Folder** from the **Edit** menu.

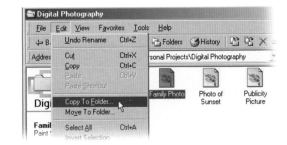

Creating a Shortcut to a Folder 40

● The **Browse For Folder** window opens.

● Navigate to the folder into which you would like to place the duplicate file, and click on the folder once to select it.

● Click on the **OK** button.

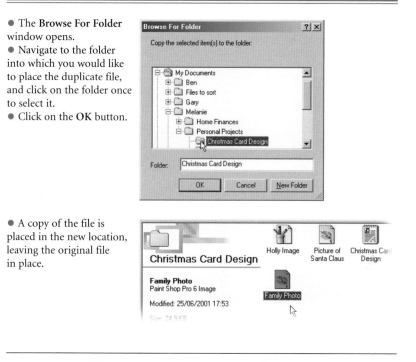

● A copy of the file is placed in the new location, leaving the original file in place.

USING DRAG AND DROP

Another way to move or copy files and folders between locations is by "dragging and dropping" them between two or more open windows. In order to do this you must first change the default Windows Me settings so that different folder contents open in independent windows, rather than opening in the same one.

1 CHANGING THE SETTINGS

● With the **My Documents** window open, select **Folder Options** from the **Tools** menu. The **Folder Options** window opens.

● Within the **Browse Folders** section, click once in the radio button next to **Open each folder in its own window**, so that a bullet appears in it.

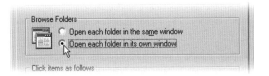

● Click on the **OK** button.

● Now, when you double click on folder icons their contents are displayed in separate windows.

● As before, select the files that you wish to move and, while keeping the left mouse button pressed down, drag the files from one window to the other.

● To copy files between locations – rather than moving them – hold down the Ctrl key as you release the mouse button.

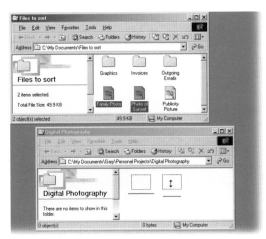

AN ALTERNATIVE WAY OF MOVING AND COPYING

Instead of using the Ctrl key to ensure that you are copying rather than moving, you can also make the choice from a menu. Drag a file into a second location using the technique described, regardless of whether you would like to make a copy or not. As you drag the file from one window to another, hold down the right-hand mouse button rather than the left. When you release the mouse button, a pop-up menu appears from which you can select either **Copy Here** or **Move Here**. It is purely personal preference, but you may want to adopt this technique until you are confident about using

keyboard commands to perform certain tasks. Note also that you can create a shortcut within your chosen location by using this method.

COPYING FILES TO A FLOPPY DISK

So far we have only made copies of files to different locations on the same hard disk. This is fine for making temporary back-ups, or if you need to use the same file for several projects, but what happens if your whole computer should develop some kind of fault that prevents you from accessing your files? Having copies on a floppy disk will mean that you still have access to those files. Or you may want to take a file to work so that you can continue working on it. Perhaps you want to give someone else a copy of one of your files. These are all good reasons why you may want to copy files to an external device – commonly a floppy disk.

1 INSERTING A DISK

● Insert a formatted floppy disk into the computer's disk drive with the metal edge facing forward and the circular metal disc on the underside. Push the disk in firmly and you will hear it snap into position in the drive.

Storage Capacity…

There are two types of 3½" floppy disk – Double Density, which can store 720KB, and High Density, which can store 1440KB (1.44MB). High Density disks display an HD symbol.

2 SELECTING THE FILES

● Open the window of the folder containing the files that you wish to copy to the floppy disk. Remember, you can change the view of the window to **Details** so that you can check the size of the files and make sure that they will fit on the disk ⬚.
● Select the files ⬚.

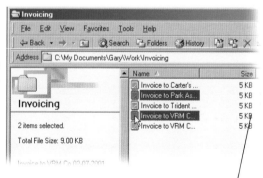

These files are particularly small and will easily fit onto a floppy disk

| 15 | Viewing Details |
| 42 | Selecting Your Files |

3 COPYING THE FILES

● With the files high-lighted, click on **File** in the menu bar and select **Send To** from the drop-down menu. You will see that the floppy disk drive appears in the submenu as: **3¹/2 Floppy (A:)**. Click once on this option.

● Copies of the files that you selected are placed on the floppy disk.

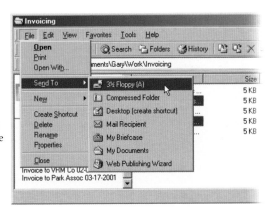

FORMATTING A FLOPPY DISK

When you buy new floppy disks, they are usually preformatted so that you can start to use them immediately. If you insert an unformat-ted disk into your floppy disk drive, your computer will not be able to recognize the disk and will display an alert message. To format a disk, select the drive **3¹/2 Floppy (A:)** from within the **My Computer** window , and click on **Format** in the **File** menu. Select the relevant options in the **Format** window to format the disk.

VIEWING THE CONTENTS OF A FLOPPY DISK

The above steps assume that you are using a new disk with maximum storage capacity. If you want to use a disk that already has files stored on it, you can view the contents of the disk in a window, just like any other drive or folder on your computer. With the floppy disk inserted, double-click on **My Computer** on the desktop. In the window there will be an icon for the floppy disk drive, **3¹/2 Floppy (A:)**. Double-click on the icon, and a window appears display-ing the contents of the floppy disk currently in the drive. From this window, you can edit or delete the contents of the disk as normal, for example, to create more storage space on the disk.

FINDING YOUR MISPLACED FILES

No matter how well-managed your filing system might be, over time you are bound to misplace some files, or forget what they are called. Because the filing system you have created is housed in one location (the My Documents folder), it is a relatively easy procedure for the computer to search for your misplaced files. To do this, you have to enter a few details about the file, and tell the computer where to look.

1 OPENING THE FIND WINDOW

● Click once on the **Start** button at the left-hand end of the taskbar.
● Select **Search**, and then **For Files or Folders** from the submenu.
● The **Search Results** dialog box appears.

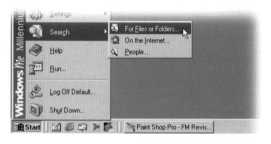

2 ENTERING THE SEARCH DETAILS

● Within the window there are several boxes into which you can enter details about the file you want to find.
● Click inside the text box next to **Search for files or folders named**. Type in a few details about what the file is called. Be as specific as possible – if you know the file name, then enter the complete name into the box. If you can't remember the name exactly, then enter as much as you can. In this example, a missing

invoice is being searched for on the hard drive.
● The next box down, labeled **Containing text**, allows you to enter specific words that you know are

contained within the file. So, for example, the invoice we are looking for here has been addressed to **Park Associates**, so this is entered into the box.

3 FINDING THE FILE

● To tell the computer where specifically to search for your file, click on the arrow next to the text box labeled **Look in**. If the filing system has been used as described so far, the file that you are searching for should be contained somewhere in the folder **My Documents**. In the list, click on **My Documents** so that it appears in the box.
● Click on **Search Now**.

4 VIEWING THE RESULTS

● Any files that match your search criteria are displayed in the window.
● Click once on a file to display its description. The details at the top of the **Search Results** panel tell you where the file is located on your computer and give additional information, such as the file size and when it was last modified.
● If you want to open the file immediately, you can easily do so by double-clicking on the file icon.

Invoice to Park Assoc 03-17-2001
In Folder: C:\My
Documents\Gary\Work\Invoicing
Size: 4,608 bytes
Modified: 26/06/2001 20:01

MAXIMIZING YOUR SEARCH SUCCESS

The more information with which you can provide the computer, the more likely it is that the files you are looking for will be found. To help, you can click on the **Date** and **Advanced** tabs in the **Find** window. Here, you can enter further information about the date when the file was created, or last modified, as well as its file type and size.

MODIFYING YOUR FILES

Now that all your files are efficiently organized, it is time to
examine the different ways in which you can modify them
to ensure your filing system is kept in good working order.

RENAMING FILES AND FOLDERS

Over time, as you expand your filing
system to include new folders and,
certainly, many more files, it will become
necessary to rename certain items.
Follow the steps below to rename both
folders and files.

1 SELECTING THE FILE

● In an open folder
window, click once on the
file that you wish to
rename so that it becomes
highlighted (you can only
rename one file at a time).
Here, we are renaming the
file that we copied from
one location to another on
page 47, so that they clearly
become different files.

File Names

Windows Me allows you
to use up to 255 characters
when naming your docu-
ments. On one hand this
is obviously a benefit,
because you can provide a
full and concise description
of your document. On the
other hand, however,
Windows will only make the
beginning of very long file
names visible when you
view your documents in
certain modes ⌐. This can
become confusing if you
have many files with a
similar beginning, so try
to differentiate file names
as much as possible –
using 20 to 30 characters.

2 RENAMING THE FILE

● Click on **File** in the menu bar and select **Rename** from the drop-down menu.

● A box appears around the current file name. If you want to change the name completely, press the [Delete] key and type in the new name. If you want to modify the name, for example, by adding to it, place the cursor at the point in the name that you want to alter and left-click.

● Rename the file and press the [Enter ←] key.

● Your file is now renamed.

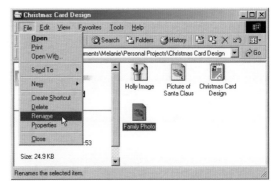

RENAME FILES WITH CAUTION!

Just as you should exercise caution when moving files ⬚, the same applies to renaming files. Changing the name of a file or folder that has not been created by you can give you and your computer a big headache when you try to perform certain functions or run applications. Limit any renaming you do to your own filing system.

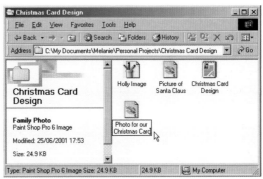

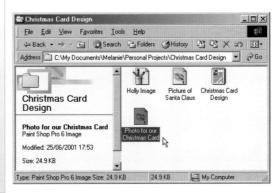

⬚ 45 **Moving Files Between Locations**

DELETING UNWANTED FILES

Deleting files from your computer is just like throwing something away – you put it in the wastebasket. Be ruthless when it comes to removing files from your computer, and only keep what you are sure you need. It won't take long for you to accumulate hoards of worthless files, including those that you believe you might *possibly* need later! In practice, you will not return to them, eventually forget what they are, and use up valuable storage space on your computer in the process.

1 SELECTING THE FILE
● In this example we are going to delete the files that are deemed not important enough to keep in the filing system. These are the files that were left in the folder called **Files to sort**. By deleting the folder you are also throwing away all the files that it contains – this saves you having to delete each file one by one.
● In the open window, click once on the folder to be deleted. If necessary, you can also use the selecting techniques ⌐ to delete many files in one process.

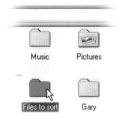

2 DELETING THE FILE
● Click on **Delete** in the **File** menu, or press the [Delete] key.

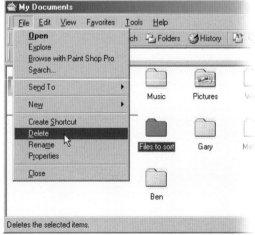

● A box appears onscreen asking you to confirm the deletion. Click on the **Yes** button.

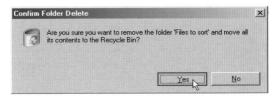

● The folder disappears from the window.
● You can also delete files by either clicking on the red cross in the menu bar (below) or dragging them to the Recycle Bin.

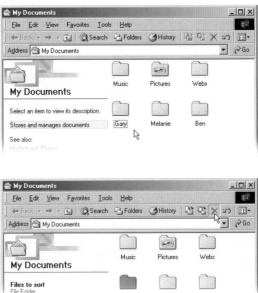

HAVING REGULAR CLEANUPS

An important part of maintaining your filing system is to have a regular review of the files stored there. If there are files that have been forgotten about, then consider whether you really need them. And if you start seeing many updated versions of the same file appearing in your folders, then you can be even more ruthless.

MANAGING THE RECYCLE BIN

Rather than deleting files immediately, the computer really moves them into the **Recycle Bin** positioned on the desktop. From this location you can restore files, so there's no problem if you suddenly realize you have made a mistake by performing the deletion. Files are only deleted permanently when you empty the **Recycle Bin.**

1 VIEWING THE BIN'S CONTENTS

● Position the cursor over the **Recycle Bin** icon on the desktop, and double-click. Notice that the icon for the bin shows that there are files contained inside it. The **Recycle Bin** window opens and displays the files you have thrown away since the bin was last emptied.

2 RESTORING YOUR DELETED FILES

● All is not lost if you place a file in the **Recycle Bin** that you later decide you need – as long as you haven't yet emptied the Bin.
● Highlight the folder that you deleted in the previous task. By selecting the folder, the entire contents of that folder are also selected.
● Click on the **Restore** button on the left-hand side of the window or select **Restore** from the **File** menu.
● The folder disappears from the window. It has been restored to the location from which you deleted it.

3 THROWING AWAY DELETED FILES

● For this task, delete the **Files to sort** folder again so that we can now dispose of it permanently.

● In the **Recycle Bin** window, click on the **Empty Recycle Bin** button on the left-hand side of the window or select **Empty Recycle Bin** from the **File** menu.

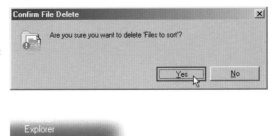

Recycle Bin

This folder contains files and folders that you have deleted from your computer.

To permanently remove all items and reclaim disk space, click:

Empty Recycle Bin

To move all items back to their original locations, click:

Restore All

Select an item to view its description.

1 object(s)

● A box appears onscreen asking you to confirm the deletion. You cannot be selective about the files that you permanently remove – clicking on the **Yes** button deletes all the files displayed in the window.

Confirm File Delete

Are you sure you want to delete 'Files to sort'?

Yes   No

● The contents of the window vanish, and the icon for the **Recycle Bin** shows that it is now empty.

Explorer

Recycle Bin

● No documents are shown in the bin, indicating that the Recycle Bin is empty

Too nervous to bin those files?

If you really can't bear to dispose of certain files then store them on some form of external device, such as a floppy disk. At least you won't be using up your hard disk space – and the files will be available, just in case!

EMPTYING THE RECYCLE BIN

You should empty the **Recycle Bin** frequently so that you do not clog up your computer's hard disk with unwanted files. However, before doing so, remember that this is your last chance to save any files from permanent deletion from your computer. Once you have emptied the **Recycle Bin**, the lost files cannot be restored.

VIEWING FILE PROPERTIES

Identical features, known as "properties," are assigned to every new file that you create on your computer, and they make the file function in certain ways. By changing a file's properties you can control the operations that can be carried out on it.

These changes include locking a file so that no modifications can be made to it (**Read-only**), hiding the file to make it invisible to others (**Hidden**), and "tagging" a file so that it is selected and backed-up automatically by your computer (**Archive**).

1 SELECTING THE FILE
● Select any file in an open folder window so that it becomes highlighted.

2 OPEN THE FILE PROPERTIES BOX
● Click on **File** in the menu bar and select **Properties** from the drop-down menu.
● The **Properties** of the file appear in a dialog box.

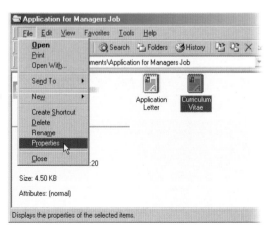

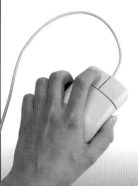

Curriculum Vitae Properties   ? X

General | Custom | Summary |

❶   Curriculum Vitae

❷ Type of file: WordPad Document
Opens with: WordPad   Change...

Location: C:\My Documents\Application for Managers Job
❸ Size: 4.50 KB (4,608 bytes)
Size on disk: 16.0 KB (16,384 bytes)

Created: 26 June 2001, 20:20:50
❹ Modified: 26 June 2001, 20:20:52
Accessed: 26 June 2001

❺ Attributes: ☐ Read-only   ☐ Hidden   ☑ Archive   ❼
   ❺

OK   Cancel   Apply   ❽

THE FILE PROPERTIES BOX

❶ *The top part of the box displays the name of the file, along with an icon* ▢ *to indicate which program it was created in.*

❷ *Here you can see what type of file it is and which program is assigned to open it (in this case, the file is a WordPad document called* **Curriculum Vitae**). *You can modify which program opens*

the file by clicking on the **Change...** button.

❸ *The location where the file is saved and its size (in this case, shown in kilobytes and bytes) is specified in this part of the box.*

❹ *This area tells you when the file was created and when it was last modified and last accessed.*

❺ *The attributes in this part of the box can be modified by clicking in the check boxes.*

❻ *Click on the* **Read-only** *option to lock your files. You will be able to open the document, but not modify or delete it.*

❼ *When the* **Archive** *box is checked, the file will be included in an automated backup.*

❽ *Selecting the* **Hidden** *option makes files invisible on your computer* ▢.

CREATING HIDDEN FILES

A hidden file remains where it is on your computer, but becomes invisible. In other words, you cannot see an icon for the file within a folder window, or its file name in an **Open** menu. This is a basic form of security because another user will not immediately be aware that the file exists. Beware though – it is a relatively simple process to display the file by anyone who knows how to make it accessible.

1 SELECTING THE HIDDEN OPTION

● Before you perform this operation, make a note of the file name because you won't be able to see it while the file is hidden.
● Open the **Properties** box for the file you that you want to hide.
● Click in the check box next to **Hidden** so that a check mark appears.
● Click on **OK** and close the **Properties** box.

2 HIDING THE FILE

● Your file only becomes hidden once you have changed the **View** options for the folder window that it appears in.
● Open the window to display the contents of the folder where your hidden file is located.

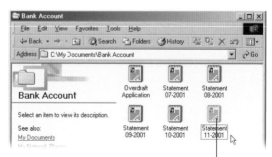

*The file is grayed-out to indicate that the **Hidden** property is applied, but it is still visible in the window*

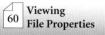

60 Viewing File Properties

● The file to which you applied the **Hidden** property may still be visible in the folder window. If it is, click on **Tools** in the menu bar, followed by **Folder Options** from the drop-down menu.

● When the **Folder Options** dialog box opens, click on the **View** tab.

● Click on the radio button next to **Do not show hidden files and folders** so that a bullet appears in the button.
● Click on the **OK** button. Now, when you view the contents of the window, your hidden file will be invisible.

3 HIDING THE STATUS BAR

● Although the file is now hidden, if the **Status Bar** is visible it will show that the file exists in the location.

The Status Bar shows there is one hidden file in the location

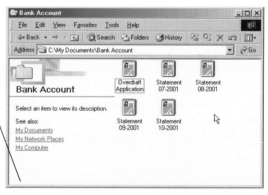

● To hide the **Status Bar** click on **View** and select **Status Bar** from the drop-down menu.

● When the menu closes the **Status Bar** disappears and there is no indication that your hidden file is saved within this location.

The Status Bar, and the information that it contained, are no longer visible

4 OPENING A HIDDEN FILE

● Launch the program in which you want to open your hidden file.
● Select **Open** from the **File** drop-down menu.

- The **Open** dialog box appears.
- Select the location of your file in the **Look in** box, then type the name of your file into the **File name** text box.
- Click on the **Open** button.
- Your hidden document now appears onscreen.

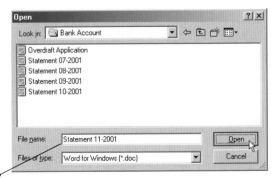

Enter the name of the file here ●

5 VIEWING HIDDEN FILES

- To make hidden files visible again, reopen the **Folder Options** box via the **Tools** menu, and click once in the radio button next to **Show hidden files and folders** so that a bullet appears.
- Click on the **OK** button to close the **Folder Options** box. Any hidden files now reappear in the window. Be aware, however, that anyone else can also follow this procedure.

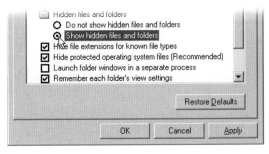

The file reappears in the window

BACKING UP YOUR FILES

Now that your filing system is in place and you are
managing your files effectively, it is time to consider
safeguarding your work against accidental loss.

WHY BACK UP YOUR FILES?

Think for a moment about all the work
that is stored on your computer. It
represents a huge commitment of not only
your money, but more importantly, your
time. If your computer should fail, or is
stolen, it will be virtually impossible for
you to recreate the documents that were
stored on your hard drive. For this reason,
creating back ups on a regular basis is
crucial. This simply involves copying files
from one location to another that is
separate from the computer itself.

PERMANENT ARCHIVES

The principal reason for backing up your
files is to insure that you have access to
them should anything unpleasant happen
to your computer or to
the original files. However,
the situation may also
arise when it becomes
very difficult or even
impossible to store any
more files on your
computer. You may have
used up your entire hard
disk space, or the volume
of files and folders on
your hard drive becomes
too unwieldy to
manage. The only
option that you're
left with may be

to remove files from your computer and
store them on an external device, such as a
CD-ROM or a Zip disk. Good practice is to
remove documents from your filing system
as you finish with them. This
should mean that there is
always spare storage capacity
on your computer, and the
backing-up process should
take a matter of minutes
rather than hours.

CREATING A COMPRESSED ARCHIVE

Unless you are regularly transferring large files to and from your computer, you may not have any device available to you apart from a floppy disk drive. If this is the case, you will need to maximize the amount of space available so that you can fit as many files as possible. File compression enables you to store many times the normal amount of files on a floppy disk by compacting them into a single "archive."

USING WINZIP

Probably the most commonly used file compression software for Windows is WinZip. If you wish, you can download a free evaluation version of this software from the internet and use it for a limited time before you have to purchase the full copy.

Visit **www.winzip.com** to download the program and follow the onscreen instructions to install it onto your computer. You will be asked a few questions in order to set up WinZip. When you are given the option, choose to run WinZip Classic – this is the simplest means of creating a basic archive file for these purposes.

WinZip has many more features than those shown below and, to appreciate its potential fully, you should treat the following steps as an introduction only. File compression is also very useful for transferring files between computers, especially if you are sending attachments by email. You can experiment with the program to see what best suits your archiving needs.

1 CREATING A NEW ARCHIVE

● Once the Winzip setup is complete, the WinZip window opens.

● Before you start, insert a floppy disk into your computer.

● Click on the **New** button at the top of the window to create a new archive.

50 | Copying Files to a Floppy Disk

2 CHOOSING THE LOCATION

● The **New Archive** dialog box opens.

● In the **Create** box, choose a location in which the archive is to be saved. In this case you can select the floppy disk directly by highlighting 3¹/₂ **Floppy (A:)**.

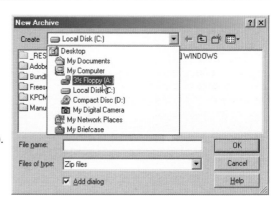

3 NAMING THE ARCHIVE

● It makes sense to create separate archive files that correspond with the names of the folders you use in your filing system.

● Decide which files you are going to archive first, and give the archive the same name as the folder where they currently reside.

● Click on the **OK** button.

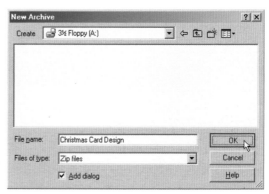

4 SELECTING THE FILES

● The **Add** dialog box opens. Select the location where the files are currently saved, and highlight them in the main window.

● Once the files are selected, click on the **Add** button.

5 THE ARCHIVE IS CREATED

● The WinZip window displays the contents of your archive file, which has now been saved onto your floppy disk.

● Close the window.

● It is now safe for you to delete the original files from your computer.

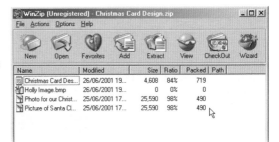

6 OPENING FROM AN ARCHIVE

● You can open the archive file by double-clicking on its icon. Then, whenever you want to open one of your archived files, simply double-click on it in the WinZip window.

● To restore files to your computer, click on the **Extract** button at the top of the window. You can then select the individual files you want to restore from the archive to your PC.

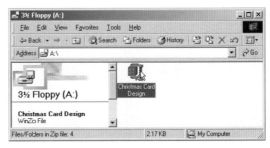

Label your disks...

File management doesn't stop there! Remember to label your floppy disks clearly to keep track of where your files are saved.

COMPARING FILE SIZES

You can see how much space you have saved by comparing the file properties ⌐ of the original folder with those of the archive file. The original files created a 54.4KB folder, whereas the archive is 2.17KB.

	Christmas Card Design
Type:	File Folder
Location:	C:\My Documents\Andy\File
Size:	54.4 KB (55,788 bytes)
Size on disk:	80.0 KB (81,920 bytes)
Contains:	4 Files, 0 Folders

	Christmas Card Design
Type of file:	WinZip File
Opens with:	⌐ WinZip Executable
Location:	A:\
Size:	2.17 KB (2,225 bytes)
Size on disk:	2.50 KB (2,560 bytes)

The size of the archive is significantly smaller ●

GLOSSARY

ARCHIVE
A file, which is usually compressed, containing back up copies of your work.

ARRANGE
To neaten or organize the icons in a window.

BACK UP
To create copies of your work on an external device, such as a floppy disk, in case you lose documents or your computer develops a fault.

COMPRESSION
The act of reducing the size of a file by using software to "compact" it into an archive.

COPY
To create a duplicate file in another location on your computer, or outside your computer, and leaving the original file in place.

DESKTOP
The screen that appears once Windows Me has started up, which displays the taskbar and, among others, icons for My Computer, My Documents, and the Recycle Bin.

DELETE
To remove a document from its current location and place it in the Recycle Bin.

DOCUMENT
A file containing user-inputted data, such as text in a Word document.

FILE
A discrete collection of data stored on your computer.

FILE NAME EXTENSION
Three letters added to the end of a file name that indicate what type of file the document is, e.g. .txt (a text file).

FILE PROPERTIES
Information about a file, such as its size and creation date, and attributes that determine what actions can be carried out on the file and how it behaves.

FLOPPY DISK
A removable disk that allows you to store and transport small files between computers.

FOLDER
A location for storing individual documents and other folders.

ICON
A graphic symbol, attached to a file that indicates its type or the program it was created in.

MOVE
To transfer a file from one location on your computer to another.

MY COMPUTER
The "entrance" to your computer. Programs, files, and access to the disk drives are located here.

MY DOCUMENTS
A folder provided within Windows Me for use as a location for saving your documents.

RECYCLE BIN
The location on your desktop where deleted files are stored. Files remain here until the Recycle Bin is emptied.

RENAME
To modify or replace the name of a document or folder.

RESTORE
To return data from the Recycle Bin to its original location.

SELECT
Highlighting files or folders to enable you to perform certain activities on them.

SHORTCUT
A link to a document, folder, or program located elsewhere on your computer that, when you double-click on it, takes you directly to the original.

STATUS BAR
The small panel at the foot of an open window that displays information about the items located there.

SUBFOLDER
A folder that is contained within another folder.

TASKBAR
The gray panel at the bottom of the desktop screen that contains the Start button, along with quick-access buttons to open programs and windows.

WINDOW
A panel displaying the contents of a folder or disk drive.

WINDOWS EXPLORER
A program for viewing and managing the contents of your computer.

WINZIP
A program used for creating and extracting compressed archive files.

INDEX

ACKNOWLEDGMENTS

PUBLISHER'S ACKNOWLEDGMENTS
Dorling Kindersley would like to thank the following:
Paul Mattock of APM, Brighton, for commissioned photography.
Microsoft Corporation for permission to reproduce screens
from within Microsoft® Windows® Me.
WinZip screen images reproduced with permission of WinZip Computing, Inc.
(Copyright 1991-2000, WinZip Computing, Inc.)

Every effort has been made to trace the copyright holders.
The publisher apologizes for any unintentional omissions and would be pleased,
in such cases, to place an acknowledgment in future editions of this book.

Microsoft® is a registered trademark of Microsoft Corporation
in the United States and/or other countries.
WinZip® is a registered trademark of WinZip Computing, Inc.
WinZip is available from www.winzip.com